Facts for Kids: 1,000 A

Facts and Trivia about Animals, Nature, Space,

Science, Insects, Dinosaurs, and more!

By: Elliot Best

Facts for Kids

African lions only catch about 25% of the prey they chase. So don't feel so bad about failure. It's natural not to win at everything.

Illness and disease can pass from a human to a gorilla.

Cheetahs are the only large cat that can't roar. They do purr a lot though.

33% of your brain power is devoted to vision.

If you travelled far enough away from Earth and had a powerful telescope you could see the dinosaurs walking around doing dinosaur stuff.

Don't eat too many carrots or your skin will turn orange!

A giant tortoise will keep growing larger until the day it dies.

Not all bones are white. Lizards can have green bones. Birds can have translucent ones.

In Japan there is an office building with a major highway running through it.

There are more than 10 trillion cells in your body.

On Pluto there is a massive heart-shaped area of ice. Perhaps this is evidence that Pluto forgives us for taking away its status as a planet. (It's now a dwarf planet.)

Spiders sometimes eat their own webs. Gross!

Geckos can bark, chirp, and squeak.

A group of cats is called a clowder.

In Japan they grow watermelons shaped like a pyramid.

The largest volcano is found on Mars. It covers an area the size of Italy.

Octopus have two arms they use to “walk” on the ocean floor. So really they have two arms and six legs.

Neil Armstrong left his space boots on the Moon.

The blades on a turbine at a wind farm are longer than an airplane.

Once upon a time, doctors thought leeches would suck an illness from a person. (They were super wrong about this.)

In the basement of the White House there's a bowling alley.

There are more stars in the universe than grains of sand in our entire solar system. And Mars is like, totally full of sand. So that's a lot of stars.

In some parts of Asia, locusts are a popular snack food.

The tree canopy in the Amazon rainforest is so thick that it takes 10 minutes for rain to trickle down to the surface after it hits the top of the trees.

Labradors are the most popular breed of dog.

Bloodhounds are so great at tracking smells that they can follow a scent that's up to five days old!

Honey never goes bad. You could eat 2,000-year-old and it would taste fine.

After the assassin bug kills its prey, it'll wear its victim's body like a Halloween costume.

Sometimes it snows in the Sahara Desert.

For about a billion years the Earth smelled like rotten eggs.

Pythons and other large snakes can swallow an entire goat.

Some scientists think our universe might be a simulation. Like a computer program.

There are about 2,000 species of insects on Earth that you can eat for dinner.

Our ears produce extra wax when we experience fear.

A giant anteater sucks up more than 30,000 insects in a day.

If a white flamingo eats too much shrimp, his feathers will turn pink.

If you put a string of pearls into a glass of vinegar, the pearls will dissolve.

The higher the dollar value on a paper bill, the longer it stays in circulation. A $100 bill circulates for 9 years.

Bears can smell food 18 miles away. So when you go camping make sure to clean the dishes or you're gonna wake up to a nasty surprise.

Humans shed a million skin cells every day. That's why there's always so much dust around!

Pandas eat 35 pounds of bamboo every day. That'd be like you eating 100 sandwiches.

Crocodiles can't chew their food. They can only rip and swallow.

If you spent one dollar every second, it would take you 32 years to spend a billion dollars.

The largest flower blooms wider than a nightstand.

A horse can be trained to paint by holding the brush in its mouth.

Newborn human babies don't make tears when they cry. Bet you never noticed that.

When a dragonfly decides to eat another insect, there's a 95% chance he will succeed. They are very efficient hunters. Not so great at dodging frogs though.

Elephant seals can dive deeper into the ocean than our best submarines.

Sneeze stuff travels 100-miles-an hour, so cover your mouth!

Traffic lights were in use years before cars were invented.

Sunflowers can grow taller than your house. The tallest one ever measured was about 27 feet.

Most people will walk 80,000 miles in their lifetime. That's about three trips around the planet.

Dracorex Hogwartsia, a horned dinosaur, was named after the wizarding school in the Harry Potter series.

Alligators go through 3,000 teeth over the course of their lives.

If your pet is in the sun too long they can get sunburned.

Jupiter weighs more than all the other objects in our solar system combined. Except for the sun of course.

Some pigs have curly hair like a sheep.

Tides are a result of the Sun and the Moon's gravity interacting with Earth.

More than 2.5 million animals take a plane trip each year.

Daydreams only last 15 seconds.

Some clouds weigh more than a million pounds. This is because they're full of water, and water is heavy!

Male donkeys are called Jacks. Female donkeys are called Jennys.

There are about 400 million dogs on the planet, and most of them are good boys!

Humans can see more than 10 million colors.

55 million years ago there were palm trees growing at the North Pole.

A frog's mating call can be heard up to a mile away.

If your dog was arrested for a crime, the police would fingerprint his nose. A dog's nose print is as unique as a human's fingerprint.

Scientists believe the asteroid that killed the dinosaurs was roughly the size of New York City.

The first brand of bubble gum was called Blibber-Blubber.

Mario (from Super Mario Brothers) was originally named Jumpman. Pacman's original name was Puck-Man.

Most animals swallow their food whole instead of chewing it.

There are at least 500,000 people flying on airplanes right now.

Sometimes sewers get clogged with fatbergs. These are giant blobs of grease.

There are more geysers in Yellowstone National Park than anywhere else in the world combined.

Poop transplants can cure serious intestinal issues.

Dragonflies can see in every direction, so good luck sneaking up on one!

Popcorn can jump up to 3 feet in the air when popped.

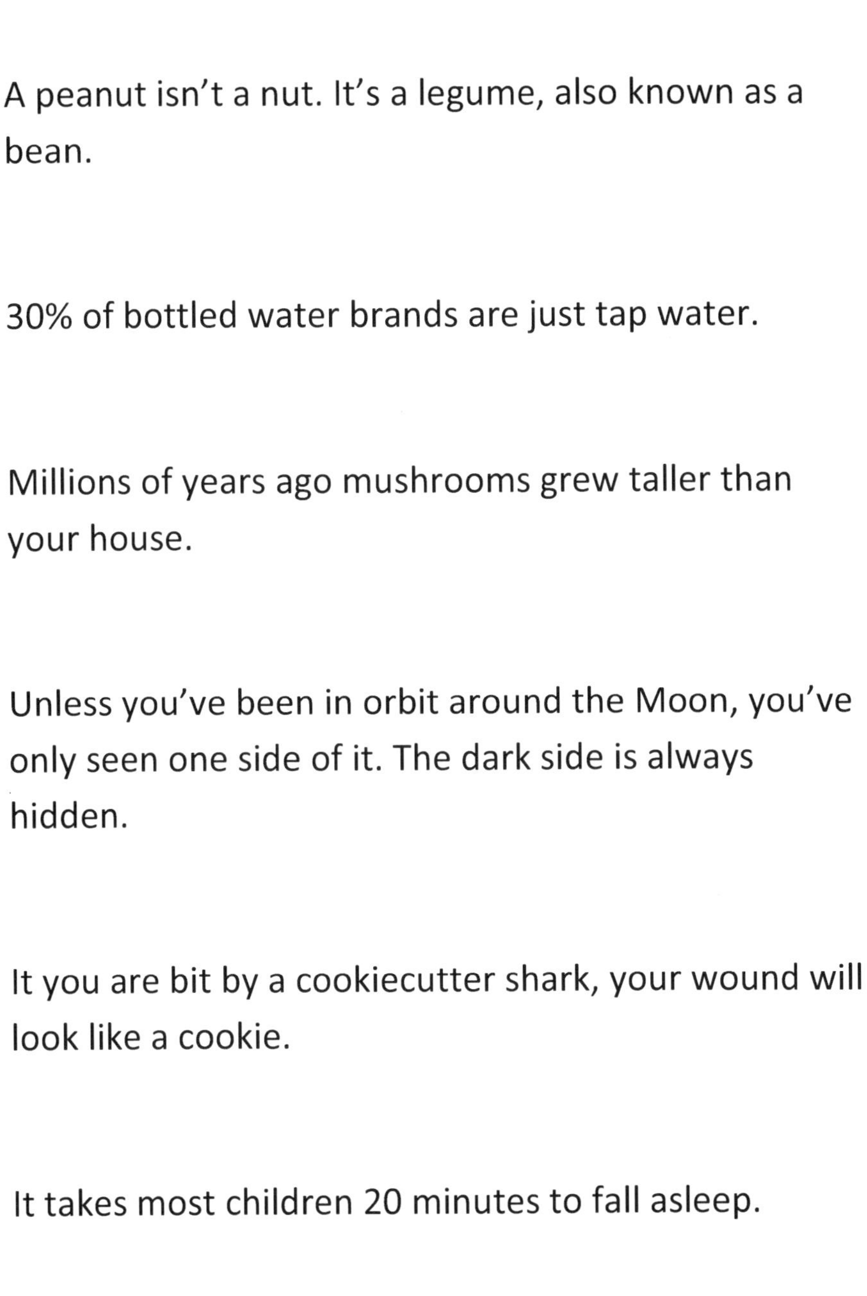

A peanut isn’t a nut. It’s a legume, also known as a bean.

30% of bottled water brands are just tap water.

Millions of years ago mushrooms grew taller than your house.

Unless you’ve been in orbit around the Moon, you’ve only seen one side of it. The dark side is always hidden.

It you are bit by a cookiecutter shark, your wound will look like a cookie.

It takes most children 20 minutes to fall asleep.

The whiskers on a catfish are called barbells.

Alaska sometimes gets as hot as Hawaii.

The world's longest footrace lasts 52 days.

The largest rodent is the capybara. It's bigger than your dog!

Love daylight? Visit the North Pole between March 21st and September 23rd. The will never set during that time.

Blue whales are bigger than the biggest dinosaurs we've ever found.

Caterpillars have more muscles than humans.

Gorillas are one of the smartest animals. They can learn to use tools, and even sign language!

It’s so cold in Siberia that your breath can turn to ice.

If a sea star loses its arms, the arm might grow a new body. Does that make them twins, or children?

Some turtles pee from their mouths.

Most bats have thumbs.

You can make a protective helmet for a bicycle out of recycled newspapers.

To tell how old a dolphin is, just count the rings on its teeth.

The dorsal fin on a killer whale is taller than most people (6 feet!)

A neurological disorder can make you slap yourself in the face. This is called "alien hand syndrome."

In Japan you can buy almost anything from a vending machine. Eggs, cars, even real estate on the Moon!

Fish can use their fins to walk on the floor of the ocean.

Australia is smaller than the Sahara Desert.

Cow farts are one of the leading causes of climate change.

Adults have about 206 bones in their body. Children have 300.

Most apes will laugh when you tickle them.

It takes up to 2 hours for a snowflake to fall from the clouds to the ground.

Tyranosaurus Rex is Latin for "Tyrant Lizard King."

If you're walking around in the forest you might come across yellow strawberries.

There are more than a quadrillion ants on Earth. That's 1,000,000,000,000,000. Humans are outnumbered 142,858 to 1. Good thing ants are tiny!

Jellyfish can sting you even when they're dead. So be careful!

Dogs were first domesticated 15,000 years ago. That's before we started building towns!

Head lice are mummified along with the body.

Orca whales can live to 105.

A Tyranosaurus Rex skeleton once sold at auction for $8 million dollars.

The heart of a blue whale weighs about 2,000 pounds.

Hummingbirds visit more than 1,000 flowers every day to keep themselves fed.

Disneyland employs hundreds of cats.

Chimpanzees can swim the breaststroke better than some humans. Lots of humans really. More than half of North America is obese these days. Obese means super-fat. Tell your friends to eat more vegetables if they want to live longer and happier lives.

Comets are just giant balls of dirt and ice. They melt a bit when they fly close to a star.

If you pay enough money you can sleep in an underwater hotel.

Half your weight is muscle.

Every golf ball has 300 dimples.

When mummifying a corpse, the brain is pulled out through the nose.

Before there was toothpaste, people used charcoal.

Flags left on the moon are slowly turning white because of exposure to the sun. It's like when you walk past a store in a small town and they've got those board games in the window that have been there forever. The colors are all faded. That's Sun damage.

Porcupines can have up to 30,000 quills. Try not to step on one.

If left in a cage by themselves, guinea pigs get so sad they can die.

In addition to mammals, both reptiles and birds also dream while sleeping.

Beaver poop is sometimes used to flavor foods.

Most people are willing to share an ice cream cone with their pet.

The most likely place for people to hide their valuables is in their sock drawer.

Light travels 900,000 times faster than sound.

Talking requires the use of 72 different muscles.

A woman ran for president of the United Sates before women were allowed to vote.

The only bird that can fly backwards in the hummingbird.

Plastic flamingos outnumber real ones.

There’s more Vitamin C in strawberries than oranges.

3D printers are useful for helping injured animals. Beaks, shells, and bones have been made to help rehabilitate animals.

Stars that burn brighter burn out faster.

Kangaroos can't hop backwards. Or maybe they just choose not to. Why don't you ask one?

Eyeballs on a giant squid are larger than basketballs.

Sharks have been on Earth longer than trees have.

Jellyfish come in different sizes, from as small as a thumbnail, to as large as a pony.

The longest earthworm is more than 100 feet.

Archaeologists once found a 350,000-year-old human footprint.

Lions can breed with jaguars and the babies are called jaglions.

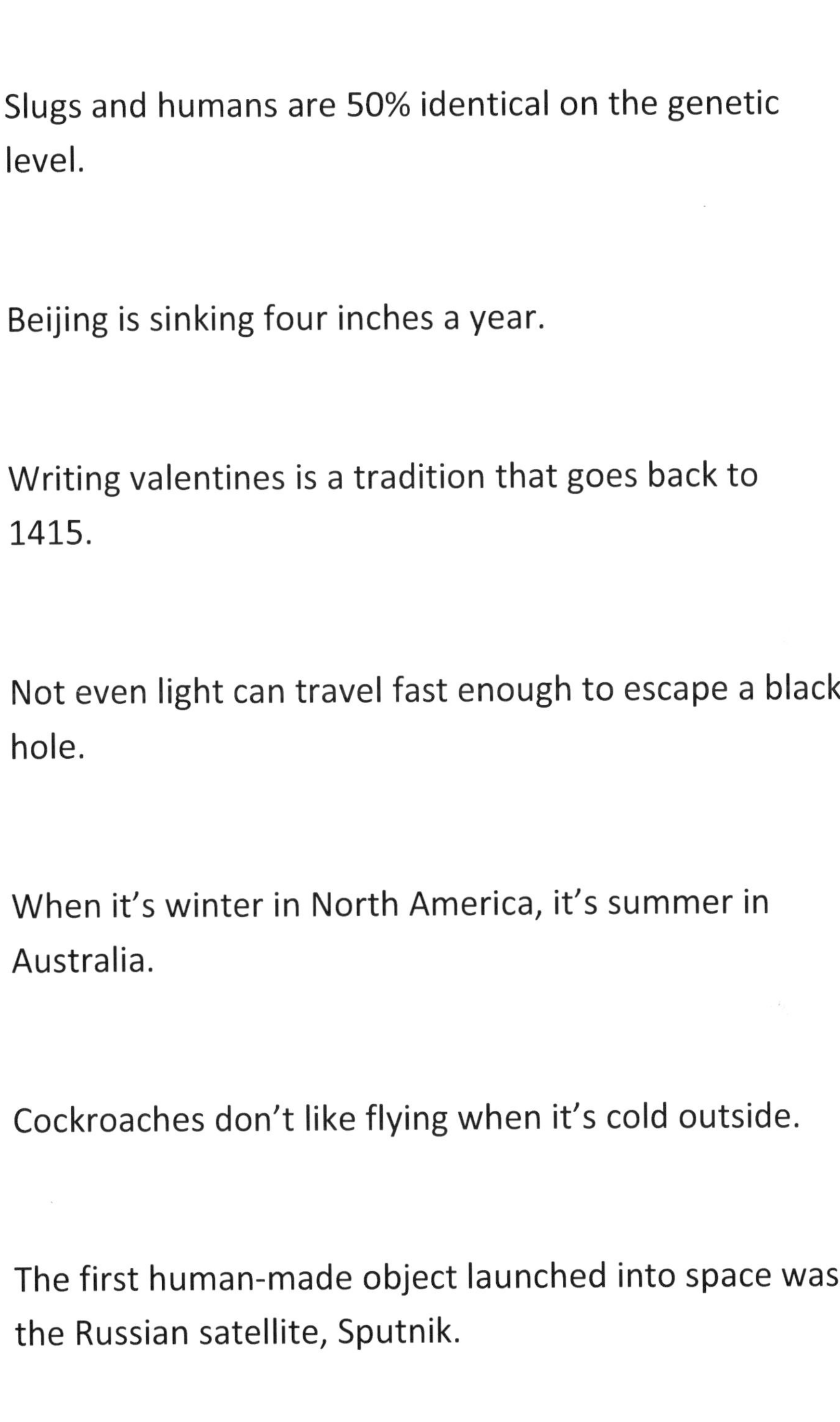

Slugs and humans are 50% identical on the genetic level.

Beijing is sinking four inches a year.

Writing valentines is a tradition that goes back to 1415.

Not even light can travel fast enough to escape a black hole.

When it's winter in North America, it's summer in Australia.

Cockroaches don't like flying when it's cold outside.

The first human-made object launched into space was the Russian satellite, Sputnik.

More than 9 trillion text messages are sent globally each year.

Astronauts bring toys with them when they go into space. Like when they wanted to test if a yo-yo worked in zero gravity. It did.

Tigers are bigger than lions. Tigers are the largest species of cat.

A green snake will turn blue after it dies. Humans turn stinky.

Fish can see more colors than humans can. Why not put your fishbowl near some art? Your fish might appreciate it.

You can't sink in the Dead Sea. You'll just float on the surface.

You could fit about 1 million planet Earths into the Sun.

Tigers hunt alone and at night. Not because they're depressed and looking for a snack, but because it's easier.

Cats cannot taste sugar.

Most gorillas will sleep in a nest, just like a bird. Much bigger though, and not always in a tree.

If you're overheated you might start yawning. This will cool your head! So try and yawn next time you get into an argument. Not only will it cool you down, the other person will think they're so wrong they're boring you.

The Pacific Ocean has more water than all other seas and oceans combined.

The Sun will burn out in about 100 billion years. Hopefully by then we'll have found a new planet to live on.

The first computers were as tall as refrigerators and took up an entire room.

The beating heart of a snake is a delicacy in Vietnam.

Giraffes like cleaning their nose with their tongue. Humans can barely touch their noses!

Christopher Columbus once thought a manatee was a mermaid. Youch.

On Mercury a day is longer than a year. It takes more time for Mercury to complete one rotation, than it does for Mercury to fly around the Sun.

The majority of kangaroos are left-handed.

The fleas on cats can't jump as high as the fleas on dogs.

Astronauts left their poop on the moon.

Some cockroaches produce milk which is more nutritious than cow's milk. Good luck finding enough to put in your breakfast cereal.

Beach sand has a melting point of 3000°F.

Most people think the first animal in space was a dog, but actually it was a fruit fly.

Some frogs eat their skin after they shed it.

Dolphins can differentiate sounds up to 15 miles away.

Women have more taste buds than men.

The regal horned lizard shoots blood from its eyeballs when threatened by predators. It's super gross, so the predators run away.

Food isn't magically safe to eat if you pick it up off the floor before 5 seconds have passed. Germs and bacteria will attach themselves to your food the split second it hits the floor.

There is a spider from Australia that can eat toads and breathe underwater. If it were any bigger we would have jettison it out an airlock.

If an animal lays an egg instead of giving birth, then the baby won't have a belly button.

The deepest hole on Earth is a cave in Croatia that's 1,700 feet deep.

If properly designed and thrown strongly enough, a paper airplane can fly 200 feet.

Snails kill more people than sharks by infecting us with a deadly parasite.

All clownfish are born as males. Some undergo a shift later on when they decide they're more of a "Barbie fish," than a "Ken fish."

In Iceland they have ice quakes.

The bones in most birds are lighter than their feathers.

It’s impossible to see a full moon and the Sun in the same sky.

Baby rattle snakes are born without their rattles.

The tallest sandcastle ever built was three stories.

It’s harder to sleep when there’s a full moon because it’s so bright. The brightness comes from sunlight reflecting off the Moon.

The common poorwill is a bird that hibernates during the winter.

The acid in your stomach is strong enough to dissolve metal. If your stomach wasn’t lined with protective mucus, your stomach would digest itself.

If it gets too hot outside, vultures will pee on themselves to lower their body temperature.

Lions spend about 20 hours a day just lying around doing nothing.

Scientists have never really agreed on how big an object in space has to be in order to be classified as a planet.

25% of the bones in your body are in your feet.

In Ancient Rome there were open-air bathrooms where people met to talk and go number 2.

The odds of a meteor crashing through your house are 1 in a trillion.

When a volcano erupts sometimes it shoots out bolts of lightning.

If a cockroach has its head chopped off it can still live for up to a week.

Dogs can hear sounds four times farther than humans can.

JELL-O used to come in celery flavor.

The holes in certain cheeses, like Swiss Cheese, are called “eyes.”

Giant kelp can grow more than two feet a day.

Tennis was originally played with your bare hands.

The Atlantic Ocean is saltier than the Pacific Ocean.

Borborygmus is the word for the groans your stomach makes when it’s hungry. The gurgling noise you hear is caused by the movement of fluid and gas in your intestines.

The African basenji (a type of dog) yodels instead of barks.

Astronauts on the International Space Station see 16 sunrises and sunsets every 24 hours.

The fear of cats is called Ailurophobia.

Your thigh bone is stronger than concrete. But don't go testing that.

Zookeepers will feed the lions popsicles made of blood when it gets too hot outside.

An avalanche can travel 100 miles-an-hour. That's a serious speeding ticket!

Toe wrestling is a competitive sport, with medal and awards.

Chickens can fly for about 12 seconds.

The smallest monkey is shorter than a pencil.

A hippo is more dangerous than a lion.

Mount Everest gets taller every year.

Sharks can catch a fish they can't even see by listening to its heart beat.

If you see a rainbow after dark it's called a moonbow.

Venus is the second planet from the sun, but it's hotter than Mercury. This is because it has an atmosphere.

Mice have more than 100 babies every year.

Cats save energy by sleeping 14 hours a day. Next time someone accuses you of being lazy, just tell them you're conserving energy and doing your part to prevent climate change.

While a cheetah might be the fastest land animal, they can only keep up their top speed for a few minutes. The animal that can run the fastest for the longest period of time can be found in your bathroom. Just look in the mirror!

Yesterday you took about 25,000 breaths. Same with tomorrow!

Stripes on candy canes are a relatively new addition. They used to be just white.

Count the rings on a fish’s scales to tell how old it is.

In Iceland you can study to become Santa’s little helper at Elf School.

A squid’s favorite holiday is Valentine’s Day because it has three hearts.

A goat will stare at you when it wants something. Staring is how they communicate.

A hippopotamus’s face is about two feet wide.

Insects sometimes form tornado-like structures 1,000 feet tall.

With the right machine you can turn sweat into drinking water.

You can still use a ripped dollar bill as long as you have 51% of it.

Woodpeckers can change color depending on the berries they eat.

Pigs can get sunburnt if they're in the sun too long.

Stretch out your arms as wide as you can. That's how tall you are!

Sharks lay the biggest eggs of any animal.

Baby sharks are called pups. Pups are abandoned by their mothers minutes after they're born.

Dolphins travel together in pods of 12.

Saturn’s rings are slowly vanishing. In a few million years they’ll be gone.

Diamondback rattlesnakes can bite you twice as fast as you can blink. So maybe don’t poke it with a stick.

Sheep have four different stomachs.

Want to increase your heart rate without exercising? Chew some gum.

Rats breed so fast that they can form a colony of millions in less than two years, and starting with only two rats.

A catfish can leap from the water and swallow a bird.

Furry Chewbacca bats were named after the beloved Star Wars character.

The largest gold nugget ever found weighed about 195 pounds. That's more than most people!

Lightning travels at a rate of 227 miles-an-hour.

The first human spacecraft to leave the solar system is called Voyager 1. It was launched in 1977 and is still transmitting data.

Ghost bats have white fur.

Ants can carry 50 times their body weight. That would be like you carrying a car on your back.

Most yawns last exactly 6 seconds.

400,000 people are born every day.

The diet of a vampire bat is 100% blood.

Gorillas carry their babies on their chest, and rarely on their back.

There are taste buds in your throat.

The world's tallest waterfall (Angel Falls) is about 20 times taller than Niagara Falls.

Grizzly bears can outrun a wild horse.

Monkey brains are a luxurious dessert in some parts of Asia.

Wolves can swim miles into the water in order to catch their prey.

An oarfish can grow longer than a city bus.

A group of otters is called a raft. A raft of otters! So cute.

Blue whales can make the loudest sound of any animal. They can be heard up to 800 kilometers away.

Millions of dollars in loose change is thrown in the garbage every year.

Fish can grow 25% in a single day if they're young and hungry. Which is how you get ahead in life.

The artist who designed Batman's cape was inspired from a drawing by Leonardo da Vinci.

The social weaver bird will construct a giant nest that houses hundreds of families. It’s like an apartment complex for birds!

Add up the opposite sides on a six-sided die and you will always get 7.

A turkey vulture can smell a rotting corpse from miles away.

The South Pole is much colder than the North Pole.

Located In Paris sewer, there is a museum about the Paris sewer system.

Some tree frogs jump from the tops of trees and glide 50 feet to the ground.

Tigers can breed with lions and their offspring is called a liger.

Chewing gum was banned in Singapore from 1992 until 2004.

Rats can survive without drinking water for longer than a camel can.

Drinks will taste sweeter when you put them in colored cups instead of white cups.

Human eyes create a teaspoon of tears every hour. Make sure to stay hydrated!

Jupiter, Uranus, and Neptune also have rings, but they're not as easy to see as Saturn's.

The top 50 tallest mountains on Earth are all in Asia.

Most cats enjoy catnip, including lions and tigers.

Australia was once just a British prison colony. People who misbehaved were sent there and forced to do hard labor.

Most countries have eliminated the 1 cent coin because it's too expensive to keep in circulation.

A camel can drink 50 cups of water in 1 minute.

City bees are harder working than country bees.

10% of Earth is covered in ice. That's a big skating rink!

It's really hard to carry a tune while holding your nose and humming.

The hottest place on Earth is Death Valley in California.

Barking pigeons have a call like an angry dog.

Jupiter has more than 63 moons. New moons are discovered every few years.

Each year humans shed about 9 pounds of skin cells.

A camel will spit on you when it feels threatened. Camel spit is also made of barf.

A scorpion can have up to 12 eyes.

Four-leaf clovers are rare, but a 56-leaf clover is even rarer! If you find one you should probably sell it on eBay.

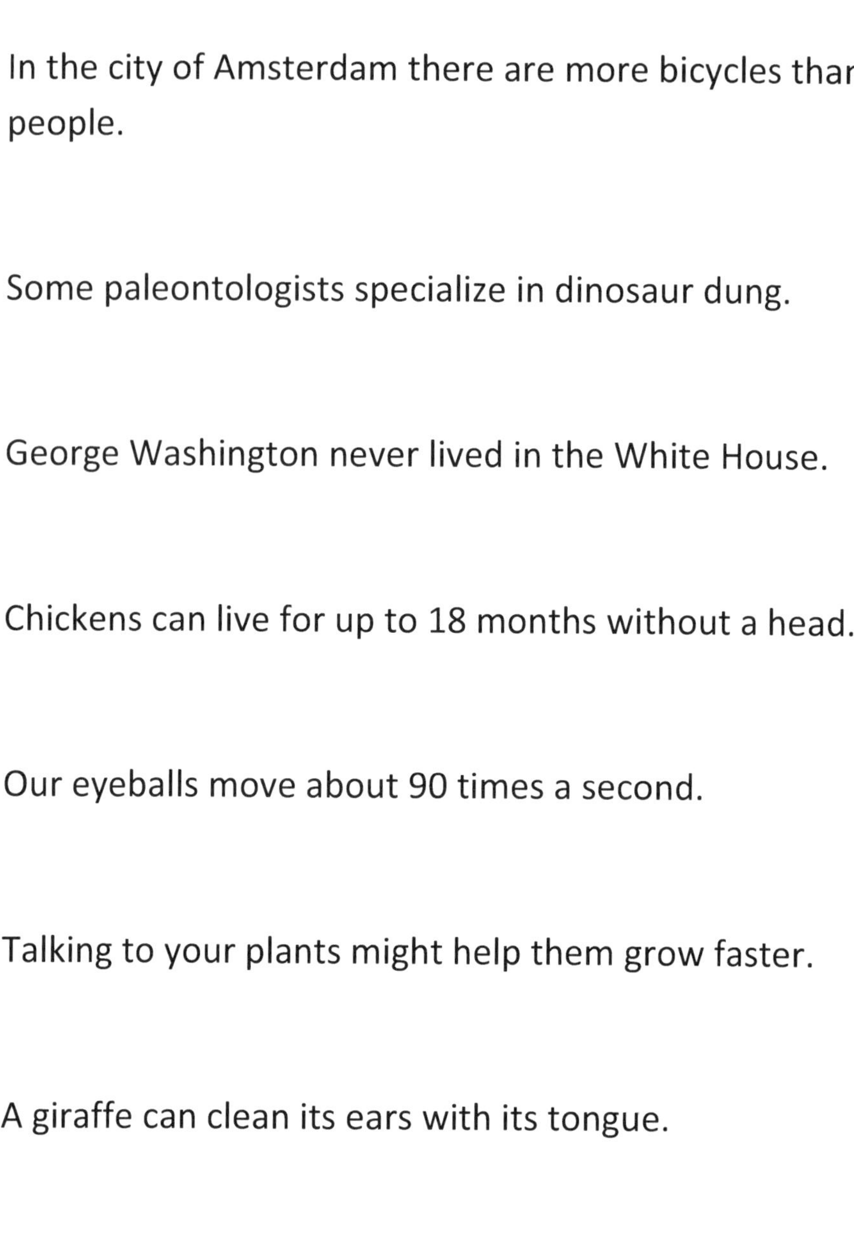

In the city of Amsterdam there are more bicycles than people.

Some paleontologists specialize in dinosaur dung.

George Washington never lived in the White House.

Chickens can live for up to 18 months without a head.

Our eyeballs move about 90 times a second.

Talking to your plants might help them grow faster.

A giraffe can clean its ears with its tongue.

The northern stargazer fish has the ability to zap things with an electric jolt.

A spacesuit weighs about 280 pounds, so you couldn't even walk around in it on Earth.

A swordfish can swim faster than a cheetah can run.

Falcons fly faster than race cars. (Obviously!)

In India, they wrap glow-in-the-dark material around the horns of cows. This is so if the cow wanders onto the road, it won't get hit by a car.

Some octopus have up to 2,000 suckers on their arms.

Panda poop can be recycled into paper.

Eagles can spot a duck from up to a mile away.

The smallest type of seahorse is tinier than a thumbnail.

Female toads don't croak, they chirp.

One teaspoon of seawater contains more than 5 million organisms. This is why scientists are so excited when they find water on other planets. Water is very important to finding life.

The world's first email was sent in 1971.

Olympic gold medals are only plated with gold. The inside is silver. 90% silver. 10% gold.

The oldest living goldfish was 43 years old.

There are 500 kernels in your average ear of corn.

Scientists have successfully grown plants in soil brought back from the Moon.

Wearing a mask on the back of your head has been shown to prevent tiger attacks.

Penguins feed their babies by barfing into their mouths.

If you stretch out your intestines the tubes are over 30 feet long.

King Tut owned a dagger with a blade made from meteorite.

The Etruscan shrew is the smallest mammal. It’s about the size of a bumble bee.

There is a hotel at the Grand Canyon that’s 200 feet underground.

Humans live on average about 2 billion seconds.

Earth is the only planet in our solar system that isn't named after a Greek or Roman god.

Giant crocodiles can survive for up to a year without eating anything.

Eels are one of the only animals that can swim backwards.

If you measure yourself in the morning and at night, you'll find that you're taller than in the evening.

Both humans and pumpkins are 90% water.

Birds don't like guacamole because they get sick when they eat avocados.

A giant octopus is born the size of a mosquito, and grows to the size of a big gorilla.

Mona Lisa has no eyebrows.

Freezing cold water weighs more than boiling hot water.

Many fish can produce a natural antifreeze in their blood.

Your brain uses less power than a light bulb.

75% of all volcanoes on Earth can be found underwater.

Asparagus used to be a popular ice cream flavor.

Geckos will bite off their own tails sometimes.

Crocodiles barf into the water to attract fish. Then they eat the fish.

Horseshoe crabs have sky-blue blood.

Rabbits can see behind themselves so it's tough to sneak up on one.

Many animals suffer from insomnia, the inability to sleep due to stress or other factors.

Hippo sweat looks like blood.

Caterpillars lose their mouths when they turn into butterflies.

The study of laughter is called Gelotology.

The killer whale is actually a species of dolphin.

Before they go to sleep, parrotfish make a bed for themselves out of mucus. That’d be like you sleeping in a bathtub of snot.

Didaskaleinophobia is the fear of going to school. Most people suffer this, especially on the first day!

The gas from each one of your farts can fill a soda can.

Egyptian mummies still have fingerprints. Even 3,000 years later!

Water bugs in Asia grow as big as your hand.

A year on Neptune is 165 years on Earth.

The world’s largest spider is bigger than a volleyball. Ick.

There is no sound in space. So when you hear an explosion in a space movie, it’s unfortunately not what you’d hear in real life :(

Some people sleep for 20 hours every day. This is called the Kleine-Levin Syndrome.

Humans can tell the difference between 10,000 different smells.

Wild turkeys can run up to 25 miles-an hour, so good luck catching one!

If you travelled back in time a few hundred years, you would notice that carrots are purple. Orange carrots are a relatively new thing.

There’s only one silverback gorilla per family. Silverbacks don’t get along too well with each other.

Gorillas can be taught to walk tight rope.

Cats and dogs have co-authored important research papers.

Many rodent species are unable to vomit.

Astronaut training involves walking underwater to simulate a low-gravity environment. They do this in pools and even sometimes in the ocean.

If a flatworm has its head chopped off it will regrow it.

Animals that least resemble a human are the scariest.

It might seem like that same fly has been buzzing around forever, but a fly's lifespan is only about 2 weeks.

You can buy a wedding gown made of toilet paper. Not sure why you'd do that, but it's nice to have the option. More options is just good economics.

20% of the food we eat is used to power our brain. It's the most important part of you. You can live without an arm, but not very long without a brain!

Pigs can jump pretty high. They can easily clear a dog.

Modern cell phone are thousands of times more powerful than the computer that flew the astronauts to the moon.

Hippos can outrun humans. They are one of the most dangerous animals in Africa.

Venus spins backwards. We believe this is because it was once hit by a giant asteroid.

Alaska is only two miles away from Russia.

Dalmatians are not born with any spots.

Tornados spin in opposite directions below and above the equator.

Some salamanders are longer than your kitchen table. Don’t pick a fight with one of these.

Bananas make your farts less smelly.

A chameleon can undergo a total color change in as fast as 20 seconds.

At least 140 species of fish can walk on land without dying.

If you wanted to push a cow over, you'd need at least 5 adult males pushing as hard as they could. But don't do this. Tipping cows is mean. If you want to tip a cow, say something nice about its hooves.

The first song ever played in space was "Happy Birthday."

Tired of winter yet? On Uranus it lasts 21 years.

Female turkeys don't gobble. Only males make that sound. Females make a clicking noise.

Dolphins are believed to be the most intelligent animal aside from humans.

Light switches have more germs on them than anywhere else in a room.

Tigers can eat up to 90 pounds of meat in a single meal.

Sea stars don’t have brains. Which is sad. Everyone should have a brain!

Algae will eat itself if it can’t find any food. (Don’t try this at home.)

The largest organ in your body is your skin.

Earth is shaped a bit like a pear. Most people think it’s a perfect sphere. But no. It’s pear-like.

Ancient humans used hollowed-out ostrich eggs to carry water around.

Manatees spend eight hours of their day just eating food.

A butterfly's ears are on its wings.

Dinosaurs might have been purple with pink polka dots. Nobody knows for sure what color their skin was.

Before the architects had finished building the Leaning Tower of Pisa, it had already started leaning.

Since there is no wind on the Moon, the astronaut's footprints are still there.

20% of people pee in the swimming pool. (Don't do this.)

The nickname for the astronaut flight simulator is called the "vomit comet."

Snakes can see you coming even though their eyelids are closed. This is because they can see through their eyelids.

Once a month Earth is hit by a meteor the size of a basketball. But every day we're hit by thousands of tiny meteorites, most of which burn up in the atmosphere.

The corpse flower only blooms once every 10 years and only for a few days. It's named the corpse flower because it smells like rotten meat.

Some lizards pee crystals instead of liquid.

Every year the president of the United States of America pardons a turkey. Instead of becoming dinner, the turkey will get to live out its life on a farm.

Anyone who says they never pick their nose is lying. Most people pick their nose about 4 times a day.

Moths can hear 15 times better than humans.

Your heart will always be about the same size as your fist no matter how big or small you are.

Each year, Hawaii drifts about 3 inches closer to Japan. Maybe one day they'll annex it!

Lions can run quickly, but only over short distances. Just like dwarves in *Lord of the Rings*.

Some lizards have a third eyeball on top of their heads.

Blue whales are as long as a ten story building is tall.

A shark can hear a fish move up to 500 meters away.

It would take 33 million people holding hands to form a circle around the globe.

If you eat too much spicy food your taste buds will die. Don't worry though they'll grow back stronger in a few weeks.

Glass bottles take a million years to decompose.

The stomach of a ghost ant is almost transparent. So you can see the food it eats being digested.

A flea can jump more than 100 times its own height. That would be like you jumping over a huge apartment building.

A tiger's stripes are at different angels on the left and right side of its body.

Cats are the most popular pet despite their disadvantage of being mostly useless around the house. There are more than 500 million cats on Earth.

Possums don't just play dead, they will also pretend to be sick. Nobody wants to eat a sick animal!

If you lose a fingernail (ouch!) it'll take six month to regrow it.

Zebra's have black skin. It's their fur that's striped.

Don't fall into a black hole, or you'll be pulled apart like warm bread.

Fried grasshoppers taste like popcorn.

Shrimp only swim backwards.

Dogs have a sense of smell that's millions of times more powerful than a human. This is how they can sniff out bombs and we can barely smell when dinner's ready.

The world record for hiccupping is 68 years.

You can buy a glow-in-the-dark wedding dress.

Birds are probably descended from dinosaurs.

Violins used to be strung with animal intestines. The material was called "catgut."

Indian giant squirrels have bright purple fur. They look like they fell into a can of paint, but nope, they were born that way.

Less than half of the wilderness on Earth has been colonized. There's still lots to explore!

Orangutans can make a simple toy whistle from tree leaves.

Newborn koala bears are smaller than a human eyeball.

The only animal with a skull but no spine is the hagfish.

If you're deeply afraid of ghosts, that's called phasmophobia.

Alligators live about 80 years, while butterflies only live a few weeks. It's not fair!

Males bees don't sting. Only females do this.

There are spiders in Australia that grow as wide as basketballs. Don't worry though, they're mostly harmless.

Along with his many daggers and golden treasures, King Tut was also buried with 20 pairs of gloves and underwear.

If you weighed 150 pounds on Earth, you'd only weigh 10 pounds on Pluto.

The first webcam was built so engineers could keep an eye on their coffee pot.

If a lady bug is scared it will squirt a smell liquid from its knees. Sort of like a skunk.

The tiny blue bird in the Twitter logo has a name. His name is Larry. Just like the cat currently living in Number 10 Downing Street.

Only 1 in 10,000 tigers are white.

A hummingbird's heart beats 1,000 times a minute. Human hearts beat around 70 to 100 times a minute.

Chickens and dinosaurs share more DNA than chickens and other birds.

You can get three gallons of oil from an emu.

There are more than 50 unique bones in a turtle shell.

The skin of some frogs contains enough poison to kill 150 people.

Most parts of the ocean are deeper than nine times the height of the Empire State Building.

Cats lick themselves instead of taking a bath. (Don't try this at home.)

If you threaten a komodo dragon it will puke in your face. You see this with humans sometimes as well. If someone of the opposite gender vomits in your face, that's generally a sign they don't like you.

Lobsters can grow as big as 45 pounds. This would cost you more than $2,000 at a restaurant.

Termites build nests using their own poop. Which is as efficient as it is unsanitary.

Dolphins are one of the only animals that can recognize themselves in a mirror.

Baby birds can breathe through their shells.

Dolphins can recognize their friends even if they've been apart for 20 years.

Sharks always have two rows of teeth. The front row eventually falls out and the back row moves forward like a conveyor belt. This process will continue until the shark's death.

Space suits cost more than $10 million dollars. So don't poke a hole in one!

1 in 10 people don't wash their hands after going to the bathroom. (Don't be this person.)

Cheetahs can accelerate up to 100 kilometers-an-hour faster than most cars.

Vampire finches are like vampire bats only much cuter.

89% of snow is simply air.

Tsunamis (giant waves usually caused by earthquakes) are very dangerous because the wall of water can be 100 feet high and travel 500 miles-an-hour.

The Chicago River used to flow in the opposite direction, until engineers reversed it.

One of the loudest natural sounds in an iceberg cracking in half.

If it's too hot outside a tadpole will switch to a vegetarian diet.

Dolphins are extremely playful creatures, and love interacting with humans.

Dogs can be allergic to cats, and cats can be allergic to dogs.

Cats have much better night vision than humans. They can see in light that's six times lower. If we could somehow get cats to team up with dogs, they would make the ultimate home security device. They could see and hear anything!

A rhinoceros doesn't sweat.

There are more than 16 million lighting storms each year.

Cats communicate with each other using a vocabulary of about 16 "words."

Snakes can eat anything up to twice the width of their head.

There won't be a full moon on Halloween until 2020.

You can train a honey bee to detect explosives, just like a dog. Bees are a little bit harder to manage though. It might sense danger and fly away!

People used to think that taking a bath would make you sick.

Some species of cactus grow so slowly that it takes 10 years to grow a single inch.

There are more insects in a small town than there are people on the planet.

The Statue of Liberty in New York, New York is covered in copper. This copper is worth at least $300,000.

In the country of Turkey there is an airport called Batman.

Earth has experienced at least 4 ice ages.

Some fish can walk across land.

Human bone is five times stronger than steel.

You can use a potato to make a simple battery.

Some prisons in Brazil employ geese as security guards. If someone tries to break in or escape the prison, the geese will honk and alert the humans.

Jackals will puke food into the mouths of their pups, just like birds.

There's 100 times as much water underneath Africa than on its surface.

You will spend 5 years of your life eating food.

Dolphins and whales sometimes have babies, and they're called wholphins.

The ears on an African elephant are shaped like the continent of Africa.

Butterflies eat food with their feet.

Aztecs used cocoa beans for money instead of coins.

Dogs and cats are sometimes elected mayor in small towns with a write-in ballot.

It would take a snail about 100 hours to slime its way half a mile.

Earth travels more than 1.6 million miles through space every day.

Pirates buying their loot is mostly just a myth. They preferred to spend it!

Fish can taste things with their tails.

Unlike other cats, cheetahs have poor night vision and can't climb trees. They also do their hunting during the day. They're quite different from other large cats!

Shaking hands spreads more bacteria than bumping fists. Some studies show up to 20 times!

New Zealand has the highest amount of cats per person. 44% of all homes have a cat. They're taking over. And they must be stopped.

Canadian gold coins are the purest in the world, and thus the most valuable.

Some sharks lay eggs.

Newborn kangaroos are no larger than a paperclip.

Elephants can cross deep rivers by using their trunks as snorkels.

Scientists estimate there are still thousands of new species in the Amazon. Insects, flowers, trees! We've barely scratched the surface.

A family of porcupines is called a prickle.

The digestive track of a giant squid is wrapped around its brain.

Female lions (lionesses) are much better hunters than males.

Turtles are older than dinosaurs.

If you've ever seen a firefly in mid-air, it was probably a male. The females aren't too fond of flying.

Moons are not all round and white. Mars has a moon that looks like a bumpy potato.

Humans know more about the surface of the moon than the bottom of the ocean.

Most earthworms have 5 hearts.

Dogs are the most popular human companion and working assistant of all the animals. Cats are mostly useless as employees. Sure they catch mice at Disneyland, but that's about it.

Sloths move so little they only burn 100 calories a day.

Jellyfish poop through their mouths.

House cats can run 30 miles-an-hour.

Of all the animals in the kingdom, pigs eat a diet most similar to humans.

The original name for The White House in America was The President's Palace. It was renamed because they didn't want to give the impression that the president was a king.

The first food grown in space was romaine lettuce. Later they grew potatoes.

A little of kittens is called a kindle. Not a Kindle, that's an e-reader!

French fries were invented in Belgium.

You can only go 10 days without sleep before dying. Sorry!

The original voices of Mickey and Minnie Mouse were married in real life.

The Venus fly trap is a flower than can eat and digest an entire frog.

Almost all of the water on Earth (97%) is saltwater.

Snakes can't slither their way across glass.

In northern places like Iqaluit, seal eyeballs are given to Inuit children as a special treat.

Some birds can remain airborne two months. They sleep while flying.

99.99% of people can't lick their elbows.

House ants smell like coconut when they're squished.

Want to know what human brains feel like? Poke some tofu.

Birds speak differently to chicks than they do to other adult birds. It's like baby-talk.

Not many things are impossible, but sneezing with your eyes open is!

The first English name for giraffes was “camelopards” because people thought a giraffe was what you get when you breed camels and leopards.

It’s hard to sneak up on a dolphin because they sleep with one eye open.

When you “smell rain” what you’re really smelling is a chemical reaction between the grass and the rain.

Your feet actually do get colder when you’re nervous. Hence the expression, “He (or she) has cold feet.”

Dogs can make more than 100 different facial expressions.

It would take a sloth an entire year to travel 12 miles.

Termites sometimes fart so strongly their stomachs explode.

You could bike to the moon if you started now and didn't stop for 3 years.

Owls are unable to move their eyeballs. They have to rotate their heads.

If you weigh 200 pounds on Earth, you'll only weigh 76 pounds on Mars.

An ostrich's eyeball is bigger than its brain. So it's probably not that bright then.

A group of blue jays is called a party of blue jays.

More than 3.5 billion people on Earth have never seen snow.

Giant clams grow as long as a bicycle.

75% of the animals on Earth are insects.

Spiders hear sounds using their legs.

Butterfly poop smells minty fresh.

Palm trees are technically grass. Their genetic code has more in common with corn than an oak tree.

North Korea doesn't like you wearing blue jeans. It's actually a crime!

While the blue whale is the largest animal ever seen on Earth, it cannot swallow anything larger than a pumpkin.

In South Africa there is a giant bullfrog that likes to pick fights with lions.

There are less than 800 mountain gorillas left in the wild.

The goliath spider has fangs longer than the head of a fork.

A group of tigers is called an ambush.

The planet Saturn is partly made of helium.

It's possible to cook food in your dishwasher, but maybe don't try this until you have your own house.

Some puppies don’t wag their tails for up to 2 months after being born.

The first pizza was delivered in 1889.

King cobras can grow 6 meters long. That’s as tall as a giraffe!

You’re more likely to get a homerun in a hot city than a cold city. Baseballs travel farther in warmer weather.

40,000 dust mites live in a single fleck of dust.

Anteaters use their tongues to grab insects more than 150 times-per-minute.

A single bee would need to visit 5 million flowers to make a single jar of honey.

Our solar system is 4.6 billion years old, while the universe is about 13.772 billion years old. So a lot of interesting stuff could have happened before humans came around.

When a gorilla is happy it'll burp to let you know.

People who play video games have an easier time finding Waldo/Wally.

Sharks don't have bones. Their skeletons are made of cartilage, like your nose.

The New Zealand lesser short-tailed bat spends most of its time looking for food on the ground. It rarely flies at all.

Bats eat about 3,000 insects every night.

Nowhere on Earth can you fry an egg on a sidewalk. It would need to be 158°F or 70°C.

Aluminum foil reduces static electricity almost as well as Bounce dryer sheets.

Garden slugs have about 3,000 teeth and 4 noses.

In some parts of the world an avocado is called an "alligator pear."

Bald eagles make nests that weigh up to 4,000 pounds.

If you drop your toast on the ground, and it's covered in peanut butter or another topping, then it's extremely likely for the topping-covered side to hit the floor. It wasn't just bad luck, it was physics!

Lightning bolts can last up to 8 seconds.

While our dreams might seem like they go on forever, most only last about 20 minutes.

Some sharks will suffocate and die if they stop moving. They swim their entire lives.

The larger the dinosaur the more likely it was to be a vegetarian.

Wearing a winter hat will make your feet feel warmer.

Cat urine glows brightly under a black light.

Race cars are so fast they can drive the length of a football field in less than second.

Bald people still have hair on their head, it's just really tiny. Microscopic actually.

Prehistoric scorpions were bigger than gorillas.

Every single drop of blood in your body travels through your heart about once a minute.

When lightning strikes, the air around it is five times hotter than the surface of the Sun.

When bears hibernate over winter they don't go to the bathroom.

The wingspan of a modern jumbo jet is longer than the first airplane flight took by the Wright brothers.

You can swim in syrup as fast as you can swim in water.

20% of people admit to dropping their cell phone in the toilet.

If you look closely at broccoli, you'll notice each head is made up of hundreds of tiny heads that each look like a big head.

The nickname for the hellbender salamander is the snot otter.

Air trapped inside icebergs can be more than 10,000 years old. So very fresh.

The average human head has about 150,000 hairs on it.

If you're trying to smell something nice, use your right nostril instead of your left. It'll smell better.

Scotland Yard is located in London, not Scotland.

Hermit crabs will sometimes use human garbage as a new shell.

Gorillas sometimes eat insects. But their diet is mostly bamboo and leaves.

The happier a cow is, the better its milk will taste. It's also more nutritious! So be nice to cows.

The only mammal that can fly is the bat. (And humans, sort of.)

Mountain lions are the only cats that can whistle.

The hooves on a horse will keep growing larger until the horse dies.

Early model cell phones weighed as much as bricks.

Hurricanes on Jupiter and Neptune can be larger than our entire planet.

The Olympic Torch has been carried to the top of Mount Everest.

There are smell receptors in our lungs.

The hairballs that lions and tigers cough up are the size of your feet.

Donald Duck's middle name is "Fauntleroy."

The rattle on a rattlesnake is made of the same stuff as your fingernails.

Belgians love chocolate so much that some of their postage stamps look and smell like chocolate.

The warmer it is outside the more likely an alligator is to hatch as a male.

Our bodies can't move much while dreaming. Thankfully!

The world's tiniest frog is smaller than a fingernail.

In China, more than 30 million people live in caves. Not like prehistoric man, of course. But nice caves. Really spacious.

Iceland has a hotel made completely out of ice. It's open all year round, even in the summer!

A lion roar can be heard from up to 5 miles away.

Sweat itself has no smell. It's only when the sweat mixes with the bacteria on your skin do you get a gross smell.

The spit from a chameleon is 400 times thicker than human spit.

Breakfast cereal has mouse droppings in it. Don't worry, not a lot.

We experience thousands of tiny earthquakes every day. They're just so small you don't notice them.

Dots on dice are called pips.

The Queen of England's crown has more than 3,000 gems.

Sloths only poop once a week.

Hair grows faster in warmer climates.

There is enough iron in your body to make a single two-inch nail.

If a gorilla is happy it will sometimes sing when it eats.

More people live in India today than the entire population of Earth 200 years ago.

Monkeys go bald just like humans.

Oysters can change from male to female depending how they're feeling.

Human babies are born color blind.

Dragonflies can breathe underwater for long periods of time.

A seagull's natural diet is fish, not garbage. Strange, but true!

Thieves in Quebec once stole $18 million dollars of maple syrup.

Toenails grow slower than fingernails.

Lions are the most social species of cat. Most cats live solitary lives, but lions prefer living in groups.

Blue stars are the hottest type. Blue fire is very dangerous. Be careful!

Some scientists think our universe might be a giant hologram.

Pluto lost its status as a planet because there are objects in its orbit with more mass than Pluto.

The first dinosaur bones discovered were thought to be dragon bones.

Cockroaches are notoriously hard to kill. They can even survive underwater for up to 16 minutes!

Most fish can't close their eyes.

Hershey made a special chocolate bar for soldiers in World War 2.

A bird's eyes can change color as it gets older.

Our brains are often more active when we're sleeping, than when we're awake.

At the center of some stars are giant diamonds.

Giraffes are born with horns. Most animals grow horns after they're born.

Some scientists think the common cold originated from camels.

The original name for Amazon.com was Cadabra.com.

It takes more strength to lift a car than pull your foot from quicksand. So watch where you step in the jungle!

Rats that listen to classical music can solve puzzles faster than rats that listen to other types of music.

Barbie and Ken (the dolls) are named after the children of Elliot Handler, one of the co-founders of the Mattel company. His children were named Barbara and Kenneth.

Millions of dust mites live in your mattress. Jump up and down on the bed to simulate an apocalyptic dust mite earthquake.

Some hurricanes are wider than 10 miles, or an entire city!

Polar bears have black skin.

The odds of getting a hole-in-one on an average golf course are worse than 1 in 12,000.

A superstorm on Jupiter has been raging for 300 years.

The largest pearl ever found in a clam weighed 14 pounds.

It's impossible to swallow and breathe in at the same time.

It would take you more than 200 million years to walk a light-year of distance.

An ostrich can run faster than a racehorse.

The record for being struck by lightning and surviving is 7 times.

Some scientists think our ears evolved from fish gills.

In India it's considered good luck if a rat runs across your feet in a temple.

Tarantulas can live for up to 20 years.

The first cell phone was priced at about $4,000.

You can make superglue from tree sap.

It took more than 70 days for Egyptians to mummify a person, but only 12 days to mummify a cat.

The original name for kiwifruit was “melonette.”

Crocodiles can’t stick out their tongues if they don’t like someone. They might try to eat them though.

Elephants can purr. They do this when they’re happy.

Salamanders can regrow arms, legs, tails, and even their eyes.

There are more than 100 billion stars in the Milky Way.

Ketchup was first used as medicine instead of a condiment.

The world's tallest tree is 380 feet tall. That's taller than 63 people standing on each other's shoulders.

House cats share 95% of their genes with tigers.

Most cats are born with blue eyes. Their eyes change color after a bit.

You can grow a pumpkin of almost any major color.

In some states in America it's illegal to sell your house if it's haunted and you don't inform the buyer. (This is an old law.)

Bottlenose dolphins have larger brains than humans.

Frogs have teeth, but toads don't.

Lobster is so delicious they even sometimes eat each other. Raw of course. They don't have access to boiling water. Not yet...

One tiny section of border between Canada and America runs through the middle of a library.

If human babies kept growing at the same rate, they'd weigh 400,000 pounds by age 10.

The Moon looks like it has more craters than Earth, but ours are just covered with vegetation.

If you take a trip to outer space, you will temporarily grow three inches.

Despite the planet being covered with millions of species of insects, only one species lives in Antarctica, the Antarctic midge. It looks like the cross between an ant and a stick insect.

There are more sheep in New Zealand than there are people.

The largest frog is bigger than a house cat.

The colder it is, the smaller the snowflakes.

Speed limits on highways are around 70 miles-per-hour. A rocket must travel 25,000 miles-per-hour to escape Earth's gravitational pull.

Elephant skin is thicker than two of your fingernails smushed next to each other.

In Australia a person with red hair is referred to as a "blueye."

The white-faced capuchin monkey says hello by trying to stick its finger up your nose.

A giant octopus can squeeze itself through a hole the size of a golf ball.

If you do karaoke with your friend and you're both singing the same song, your heartbeats will synchronize.

A black hole can eat an entire star.

Flying vampire frogs only have fangs when they're tadpoles.

The average dairy cow produces about 100,000 glasses of milk during its life.

All species of frogs have a unique croak and mating call.

In Australia there is a lake that is totally pink.

Mosquitos prefer human blood to animal blood.

300 million emails are sent every minute.

Elephant boogers are bigger than apples.

Mice, dogs, chimpanzees, guinea pigs, monkeys, and humans are the only species (aside from various insects) to have flown in space.

Earth's largest mountain range is under the sea.

Human babies will start yawning before they're born.

Jellyfish can have tentacles that stretch longer than a gymnasium.

Some volcanoes are always erupting. One in Italy has been erupting for 2,000 years.

On some planets it rains glass and metal.

When McDonald's first opened in Kuwait, the line up to get inside was 7 miles long.

The praying mantis is the only insect that can peer over its shoulder.

Some fish can change from female to male if there aren't enough males around.

The lights on the casinos in Las Vegas are so bright you can see them from up to 250 miles away.

The Great Wall of China is almost as long as Africa.

To stay cool, kangaroos lick their forearms.

The largest living structure on Earth is the Great Barrier Reef in Australia.

Humans fart about 15 times a day.

The word purple comes a Greek word for shellfish.

You can turn fish scales into lipstick and nail polish. (This fish does not survive this process.)

You will blink more than 17,000 times every day. Don't try and count them or you'll fall asleep!

20% of all the fresh water on the planet is in a lake in Siberia.

Sharks are believed to be color blind.

The longest-living organisms on Earth are trees.

There are about 180,000 words currently in use in the English language, and about 48,000 obsolete words.

Pacman's first design had him looking like a pizza with slices removed for his mouth.

Some types of chickens lay green eggs. And blue ones.

The Chihuahua is the smallest breed of dog.

The only province, state, or territory in North America with the letter Q in its name is Quebec.

Koalas sleep 20 hours a day.

You can get cell phone reception on the top of Mount Everest, but not in many rural communities in Canada. What's up with that?

Some species of piranha are vegetarian.

If you cross a donkey and zebra you get a zedonk.

If a frog is big enough it will eat a crab.

Mars is smaller than the Earth's core.

The first ice skates were made with bones. This was 4,000 years ago!

Some flowers and trees are so toxic that standing underneath them while it's raining could kill you.

Only female mosquitos will bite you. The males are much nicer.

Baseball pitchers will sometimes spit on the ball before they throw it. This makes it harder to hit. It's also gross. And against the rules.

A lobster's teeth can be found in a pretty strange place; it's stomach!

Forest fires travel twice as fast uphill as downhill.

A male ostrich can roar as loud as some lions.

The national animal in Scotland is a unicorn.

Honeybees can lift almost their entire bodyweight in pollen.

Female lions prefer males with darker manes.

The bigger the fish tank, the larger your goldfish will grow. In the open water they can get up to two feet long.

There are more redheads in Ireland than anywhere else on the planet.

Coyotes can hear mice scurrying under a foot of snow.

In the middle ages, children were sewn into their clothes so they would stay warm during winter.

Ancient Romans used crocodile poop to soften their skins and get themselves uninvited to future parties.

The tongue of a chameleon is longer than its body.

Each year has more than 31.5 million seconds in it.

Crocodiles can digest human bones. So try not to get eaten by one. If a crocodile bites you, punch him in the eyeballs. It might shock him into letting go. Like Mike Tyson said, “Everyone has a plan until they get punched in the face.”

Made in the USA
Middletown, DE
20 December 2019

81386964R00071